NOV 13 2017

3 1994 01566 0969

SANTA ANA PUBLIC LIBRARY

AR PTS: 1.0

D0760857

J 940.53 HUT
Hutchison, Patricia
World War II

$31.35
CENTRAL   31994015660969

WORLD WAR II
12 THINGS TO KNOW

by Patricia Hutchison

12 STORY LIBRARY

Tensions Rise in Europe and the Pacific

World War I ended in 1919. It was called "the war to end all wars." But it did not live up to its name. The war left many countries in ruins. Their governments were weak. A new political system rose up out of the ashes. It was called fascism. Dictators came to power in Italy, Japan, Germany, and other countries. They promised to make their countries mighty again. The most powerful fascist leader was Adolf Hitler.

Hitler became the chancellor of Germany on January 30, 1933. With his Nazi Party, he created a strong police force. He also built up a large army. Hitler wanted to gain more land for Germany. His army began to invade other countries.

Great Britain, France, and Italy signed the Munich Agreement with Germany in September 1938. The deal gave Germany control of land in western Czechoslovakia. In return,

THINK ABOUT IT

Find out more about the causes of World War II. Which do you think was the most important? Give reasons for your answer.

6

Number of months Hitler kept to the terms of the Munich Agreement.

- In 1933, Hitler became the dictator of Germany.
- Hitler began to build up Germany's armed forces.
- In 1938, Germany signed the Munich Agreement.
- Hitler agreed not to claim more territory.
- In March 1939, Hitler invaded Czechoslovakia, breaking the Munich Agreement.

Great Britain, France, United States, Soviet Union, and their allies

Germany and its allies

Neutral

Controlled by Germany and its allies

This map shows the parts of Europe Germany controlled throughout World War II.

Hitler said he would not use force to take over the rest of the country. But in March 1939, Hitler broke the terms of the Munich Agreement. The German army moved into Czechoslovakia. Then, Hitler set his sights on Poland. The British government vowed to help the Polish people if Hitler attacked them. The British feared Germany would try to take over more of Europe.

War Begins as Hitler Invades Poland

On September 1, 1939, German forces bombarded Poland. Adolf Hitler wanted to rule there, too. British leaders kept their promise to the Polish people. They declared war on Germany two days later. France was another ally of Poland. It also declared war on Germany. World War II had officially begun.

Hitler did not want a long war. He used a new military strategy. It was called the *blitzkrieg*, or "lightning war." Hitler lined up his armies along a narrow piece of land. His ground and air forces stormed enemy lines. Then, German tanks drove in. They roamed freely behind the lines. This caused chaos for Germany's opponents. They were easily defeated.

Hitler's blitzkrieg swept through nine European countries in nine months.

On September 1, 1939, 62 German divisions and 1,300 aircraft invaded Poland.

THE PHONY WAR

For nine months after Hitler invaded Poland, Great Britain and France did little fighting with Germany. This period became known as the "Phony War." British bombing raids over Germany dropped leaflets instead of explosives. The leaflets explained the evils of the Nazi Party. The Phony War came to an end in May 1940, when Hitler invaded France.

2

Number of days from the time Germany invaded Poland until World War II began.

- On September 1, 1939, Germany invaded Poland.
- Great Britain and France declared war on Germany on September 3. This was the start of World War II.
- Hitler's security force began to kill anyone who disagreed with Nazi beliefs.

They included Denmark, Belgium, and Greece. He invaded France in May of 1940. By April 1941, he had captured much of Europe.

Germany invaded Belgium on May 10, 1940.

Hitler set up a security force, or SS, in each country. They began to kill anyone who disagreed with their Nazi beliefs. People began to fear the SS, especially people of the Jewish faith. Hitler hated the Jews. He wanted to wipe them out entirely. He would stop at nothing to get rid of them.

Axis Powers Line Up for War

Adolf Hitler made two important alliances in 1936. The first was a pact with Italy. The other was an alliance with Japan. The three countries joined forces to become the Axis powers in 1940. They signed an agreement called the Three-Power Pact. All three countries wanted to become large, powerful empires. Their leaders promised to help each other claim new lands as their own. They also vowed to destroy the Soviet Union. It was a communist country. The Axis powers wanted to rid the world of communism.

As part of the Three-Power Pact, the countries' leaders were partners. Germany's Adolf Hitler worked with Italy's leader, Benito Mussolini, and Japan's leader, Emperor Hirohito.

According to the pact, each of the leaders would be the supreme ruler of his own land. The leaders would never attack each other.

Other nations in Europe followed suit and became Axis members.

Adolf Hitler (right) admired Benito Mussolini (left) as a leader. The two men met for the first time in 1934.

Emperor Hirohito (right) held the throne from 1926 to 1989. He was Japan's longest-reigning emperor.

3

Number of major leaders in the Axis powers.

- Germany, Italy, and Japan signed an alliance agreement in 1940.
- Their goals were to make their countries powerful, claim more land as their own, and destroy the Soviet Union.
- Within one year, six other countries joined the three main Axis powers.

Hungary was the first to join the three main Axis powers. Soon, Romania entered the alliance. Bulgaria, Yugoslavia, and Croatia also joined the union. By June 1941, nine countries belonged to the Axis.

4

Japan Bombs Pearl Harbor

President Franklin Delano Roosevelt wanted to help when World War II broke out. But most Americans wanted to stay out of combat. The United States lost more than 100,000 men in World War I. It did not want to take part in another battle. Instead, it loaned weapons to countries fighting against Germany. It hoped Germany would be defeated. In December 1941, many Americans changed their minds about taking part in the war.

On December 7, 1941, at 7:55 a.m., Japanese planes appeared in the sky over Pearl Harbor, Hawaii. They bombed US airfields and attacked navy ships. Smoke and

More than 1,000 men were inside the USS *Arizona* when it exploded and sank.

flames billowed from the crippled ships. Some sailors dove into water covered in burning oil. Others were bleeding from bullet wounds. Some had broken limbs. Many died.

When the bombing ended, many US ships were sunk or badly damaged. The Japanese had killed thousands of people. Americans were shocked. They feared Japan might attack the US mainland.

The next day, President Roosevelt gave a speech to Congress. He said December 7 was "a date which will live in infamy." Many people now felt the country had no choice but to take part in the war. That day, the United States declared war on Japan. On December 11, Germany and Italy declared war on the United States. The conflict became a true world war.

2,471
Number of Americans killed at Pearl Harbor.

- On December 7, 1941, the Japanese bombed Pearl Harbor, Hawaii.
- On December 8, the US Congress declared war on Japan.
- Germany and Italy declared war on the United States on December 11.
- The war became a true world war.

President Roosevelt signed the declaration of war against Japan at 4 p.m. on December 8.

Allied Powers Prepare to Fight Back

The Axis powers waged a bloody war on the world. They began invading other countries. Those that opposed the Axis fought back. They created the Allied powers. The main Allied powers were the United States, Great Britain, the Soviet Union, and France. Their leaders were Franklin Roosevelt, Winston Churchill, Joseph Stalin, and Charles de Gaulle.

The Allies wanted to restore peace. But each leader had a different idea of what that meant. Roosevelt wanted to end fascist governments. He wanted to spread democracy throughout the world. Churchill wanted to crush Germany and prevent it from rising again. Stalin also wanted to quash Germany.

Leaders Winston Churchill (left), Franklin Delano Roosevelt (center), and Joseph Stalin (right) worked together during World War II.

France had fallen to Hitler. De Gaulle wanted to win France back.

The United States, Great Britain, and the Soviet Union worked together. They made battle plans. They worked to free France and other countries under Hitler's control. They were determined to win the war against Hitler and the Nazis.

Germany took control of Paris, France, on June 14, 1940.

4
Number of major Allied powers.

- The United States, Great Britain, the Soviet Union, and France were the major Allied powers.
- The Allied leaders were Franklin Roosevelt, Winston Churchill, Joseph Stalin, and Charles de Gaulle.
- The Allies wanted to restore peace.
- The United States wanted to spread democracy.

ALLIES ACROSS THE GLOBE

The Allies were made up of more than 26 countries. They came from six continents. Canada, Mexico, Bolivia, and Brazil were a few of the countries that joined from the Americas. In addition to Great Britain and France, eight other European countries helped out. From Asia, China, India, and the Philippines took part. South Africa and Ethiopia joined the Allies as well.

Soldiers Ship Out Overseas

Almost 6 million Americans volunteered to serve in the army, navy, and army air force. By law, men between the ages of 21 and 45 had to register to serve in the military. This was called the Selective Service System, or the draft. Of 50 million men who registered, 10 million were drafted in World War II. By 1945, a total of 16 million men had served in the war. Most were sent to fight battles in Europe and the Pacific.

The army used rifles, machine guns, rocket launchers, and tanks. Navy aircraft carriers became major weapons. These ships launched planes into the air from a very short flight deck. The planes carried bombs, rockets, torpedoes, and machine guns. Army air force pilots flew strike aircraft. They used heavy firepower to battle at close range.

First Lady Eleanor Roosevelt and many women's groups urged US leaders to allow women to serve in the military. On May 15, 1942,

The US Coast Guard entered the war in 1941.

Congress formed the Women's Army Corps, or WAC. Women were not allowed in combat. They worked military jobs in the United States and overseas. Members of the Army Nurse Corps tended to wounded soldiers. The Navy's Women Accepted for Volunteer Emergency Services (WAVES) provided support at home. The Women's Airforce Service Pilots (WASPs) became the first women to fly US military aircraft. Specially trained flight nurses helped transport wounded men from battle lines to hospitals.

Posters encouraged women to join the WAC.

Are you a girl with a Star-Spangled heart?

JOIN THE WAC NOW!

THOUSANDS OF ARMY JOBS NEED FILLING!

Women's Army Corps
United States Army

73
Percentage of the US military sent to fight battles overseas.

- During World War II, 16 million Americans served in the military forces.
- Approximately 6 million men volunteered, and millions more were drafted.
- Soldiers used a variety of weapons on the ground, in the air, and on the sea.
- Approximately 350,000 women volunteered for military service.

THINK ABOUT IT

How have women's roles in war changed since World War II? Write down three things women today can do to help with war efforts that they could not do in the 1940s.

Life Changes Almost Overnight for US Citizens

Fear gripped the country after the Japanese bombed Pearl Harbor. People dreaded an attack on the US mainland. They soon realized they would have to sacrifice in order to win the war against the Axis powers.

Ration stamps were issued in the spring of 1942. Families used them to buy limited amounts of gas, food, and clothing. Communities held drives for tin cans and rubber tires. These items were recycled to make weapons and bullets. People bought bonds to help pay for the war.

The United States needed huge numbers of planes, tanks, rifles, and warships. Factories that made toasters and other appliances began to make guns and tanks. Many men served in the military. This left a gaping hole in the workforce. Women began to fill in. They became welders and electricians. Before the war, these jobs were for men only.

Life changed even more for many Japanese Americans. Some people thought they might help Japan invade the United States. As a result, President Roosevelt signed Executive Order 9066. The law called for nearly 120,000

Women work at an aircraft plant in 1941.

A Japanese family in the United States on its way to an internment camp

Japanese Americans to be removed from their homes. They were sent to live in internment camps along the West Coast. Even Japanese Americans who were born in the United States were forced to live in these prison camps surrounded by barbed wire and armed guards.

THINK ABOUT IT

What are some ways you might have helped on the home front during the war? Write down three things you could have done.

10

Approximate percentage of increase of women in the workforce during World War II.

- Rationing programs limited the amount of food, gas, and clothing people could buy.
- Scrap metal and rubber were recycled into weapons.
- Women did jobs that had mostly been performed by men.
- Japanese Americans were put in internment camps.

Battle of Midway Rages in the Pacific

After Japan's victory in the surprise attack on Hawaii, it decided to try to sink more US aircraft carriers. The Japanese fleet commander chose to strike Midway Island. The plan was to draw out the US fleet. When it tried to fight back, Japan would destroy it.

But US intelligence agents picked up important Japanese messages. Early in May 1942, code-breakers figured out an attack was going to take place. By mid-May, they knew when and where it was going to happen.

The Pacific Fleet commander put US carriers in place to surprise the Japanese. Four Japanese aircraft

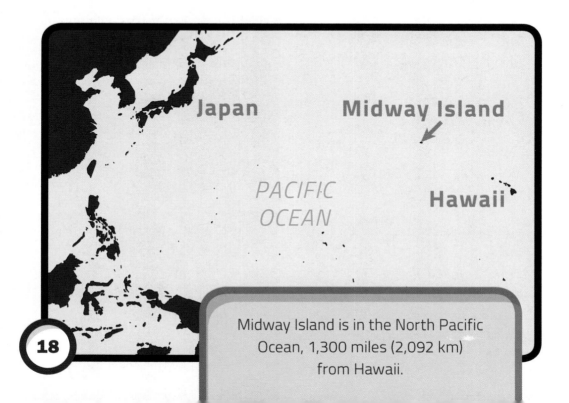

Japan

Midway Island

PACIFIC OCEAN

Hawaii

Midway Island is in the North Pacific Ocean, 1,300 miles (2,092 km) from Hawaii.

Aircraft prepare to attack Japanese carriers on the first day of the Battle of Midway.

carriers attacked the US base on Midway on June 4. When they were returning to refuel, they found the US fleet ready for battle. US bombers attacked the fleet and left it badly damaged. They continued the strikes for two days. The Japanese suffered heavy losses. Finally, they gave up and drew back to Japan.

The US victory at Midway was a turning point in the war in the Pacific. It stopped Japan's forward movement. The Allies began to take an offensive position in the war against Japan.

4

Number of Japanese aircraft carriers that attacked Midway Island.

- In June 1942, the Japanese attacked the US military base at Midway Island.
- US forces knew the Japanese were going to strike.
- The United States put carriers in place to fight back.
- The Japanese suffered heavy losses.
- The US victory at Midway Island was a turning point in the war in the Pacific.

19

Battle of Stalingrad Ends in German Defeat

The war in Europe raged on. Hitler and the Axis powers continued to sweep eastward. On June 22, 1941, the Germans began Operation Barbarossa. Their goal was to invade the Soviet Union. More than 3 million Axis troops took part. There were 3,500 tanks. The Soviets were not ready for the attack. The Germans quickly gained ground. They killed or captured more than 900,000 people. But the Soviets were not ready to give up.

Winter blew in, causing frigid temperatures. German soldiers were freezing. They backed off until the weather warmed. This gave both sides time to ramp up with more men and more power.

The Battle of Stalingrad took place between 1942 and 1943. In September 1942, the German army marched outside of Stalingrad, Russia, which was part of the Soviet Union. The Germans expected to quickly take over the city. But the Russians felt differently. They began to fight back. Months later, the battle was still raging. The Germans were running out of men and weapons. The Soviet Red Army circled around them.

HOLOCAUST IN GERMANY

While Hitler's troops were fighting in Russia, the Holocaust was taking place in Germany and other European countries. Jews lived in fear of Hitler's SS. SS officers had absolute power. They rounded up Jews and sent them to ghettos. There, they lived in crowded, filthy conditions. Later, the SS sent Jews in cattle cars to concentration camps. Many died of starvation and disease. Millions were killed in gas chambers.

Hitler told his men to hold their ground at all costs.

When winter arrived, many Germans starved to death. Approximately 150,000 died. Only 91,000 remained. Finally, on February 2, 1943, the Germans surrendered. The Allies had defended Stalingrad.

The Battle of Stalingrad was one of the bloodiest in history. But it was a turning point in the war. The Allies stopped the Germans' advance into the Soviet Union. Hitler was disgraced. Stalin gained confidence. He began to move his troops westward toward Germany.

2 million
Number of soldiers who were killed or wounded in the Battle of Stalingrad.

- Hitler expected to win quickly in the Soviet Union.
- The Germans began to run out of men and food.
- The Germans surrendered after five months of fighting.
- The Allies stopped Germany from taking over the Soviet Union.

The Battle of Stalingrad was a major win for the Allies.

D-Day Leads to Victory in Europe

In 1943, Allied forces were gathering in Great Britain. Hitler suspected they would attack the coast of France. But Hitler did not know where the invasion would take place. In November, Hitler ordered his troops to finish building the Atlantic Wall along the coast of Europe. It was made up of more than 2,400 miles (3,862 km) of trenches, bunkers, and land mines.

Operation Overlord began on June 6, 1944. At dawn, thousands of Allied paratroopers landed behind enemy lines. They secured bridges and roads. Soon, the Allied forces landed on the beaches of Normandy, France. They came in 5,000 ships and landing craft. The men ran through the water and onto the beach. Nearly 11,000 aircraft gave them cover overhead. Many lost their

Ships brought cargo to Omaha Beach during Operation Overlord.

May 8 is Victory in Europe Day. It celebrates the day German soldiers laid down arms.

150,000

Number of Allied troops that landed in Normandy on D-Day.

- Hitler built up a defense zone along the coastline of western Europe.
- On June 6, 1944, Allied forces invaded Normandy in Operation Overlord.
- Paris was freed from German control in August 1944.
- On May 7, 1945, Germany surrendered.

lives storming the Atlantic Wall. It was one of the largest land, air, and water raids in history.

The beaches were fully secured one week later. The Allies continued to advance. At the end of August, they reached Paris. France was freed.

The invasion, also called D-Day, was the beginning of the end for Hitler. Allied forces moved eastward toward Germany. Soviet troops moved westward. The Nazis were squeezed in the middle. Hitler committed suicide on April 30. On May 7, 1945, Germany surrendered.

PREPARING FOR D-DAY

Operation Bodyguard took place before the D-Day invasion. Allies set up phony military forces 150 miles (241 km) northeast of Normandy. They used pretend aircraft and ships, inflatable tanks, and dummy paratroopers. The plan was to fool the Germans. It worked. It was weeks before they sent more troops to Normandy.

US Bombing Causes Japan to Surrender

Japan was nearly defeated by the summer of 1945. Its navy and air force were ruined. Bombings left the country in shreds. The Allies planned an attack on mainland Japan. It was set for November 1945. Officials knew the invasion would be bloody. Many lives would be lost on both sides.

On July 16, the United States tested a new weapon. They secretly exploded the world's first atomic bomb in the desert of New Mexico. The Potsdam Declaration was issued 10 days later. It said Japan's armed forces would be completely destroyed and their homeland would be ruined if they did not surrender. Japan's prime minister paid no attention to the threat. On August 6, a US B-29 bomber dropped an atomic bomb on Hiroshima, Japan. Tens of thousands of people were killed instantly. Thousands more died later from wounds, burns, and exposure to radiation.

Japan still resisted surrender. Meanwhile, the Soviet Union attacked Japan in Manchuria. On August 9, the United States dropped a second atomic bomb, on Nagasaki. Japan's leaders continued

Mushroom cloud from the bombing of Nagasaki, Japan

80,000

Estimated number of people instantly killed in the bombing of Hiroshima, Japan.

Japanese officials signed the surrender documents on September 2, 1945.

- The Allies planned to invade mainland Japan in November 1945.
- The first atomic bomb was exploded in New Mexico.
- The Allies warned Japan to surrender or its army would be destroyed and homeland would be ruined.
- The United States dropped atomic bombs on Hiroshima and Nagasaki, Japan.
- Japan surrendered on August 15, 1945.

to debate. They wanted their emperor to remain in power. Finally, on August 15, 1945, Emperor Hirohito gave a speech on national radio. He announced the surrender of Japan. The United States accepted right away. World War II was finally over.

High Price of War Takes Its Toll

More than 50 countries fought in World War II. The entire world felt the war's impact. World War II was the bloodiest war in history. More than 55 million people died. Millions more were injured. Many countries lost more than 10 percent of their populations. Many people lost their homes and everything they owned.

Six million European Jews were killed in the Holocaust during World War II. Hitler believed the Jews worked to keep Germany from winning World War I. He felt they were dangerous to German society. Jews were forced to live in camps and perform slave labor. Many were shot or gassed to death. Others died from starvation and diseases.

World War II was the most expensive war in history. The total cost was between $1 trillion to $2 trillion. The United States alone spent 10 times more than it had in all its earlier

Brazilian soldiers in Italy in 1944

wars put together. Property damage totaled more than $239 billion.

Before the end of World War I, Germany and Japan had been leaders in their parts of the world. World War II left these countries in ruins. Positions of leadership were left empty. The Soviet Union saw this as a chance to share its ideals. Communism spread throughout Europe and Asia. Tensions rose between democratic and communist nations. This friction would last for years to come.

World War II Memorial in Washington, DC

6 million
Number of Jews killed by the Nazis.

- More lives were lost than in any other war.
- World War II was the most expensive war in history.
- The war cost between $1 trillion to $2 trillion.
- After the war, the Soviet Union spread communism to many countries.

GERMAN LEADERS TRIED FOR THEIR CRIMES

The Nuremberg trials began in October 1945. German leaders were charged with war crimes and crimes against humanity. These included the killing of millions of Jews, the disabled, and other minorities. Many men were hanged for their offenses. Others committed suicide before they could be executed.

12 Key Dates

January 30, 1933
Adolf Hitler becomes the chancellor of Germany.

September 1, 1939
German forces invade Poland.

September 3, 1939
Great Britain and France declare war on Germany.

December 7, 1941
The Japanese bomb Pearl Harbor, Hawaii.

May 15, 1942
The US government creates the Women's Army Corps.

June 4, 1942
Japanese forces blast Midway Island.

February 2, 1943
The Germans surrender in the Battle of Stalingrad.

June 6, 1944
Allied forces conduct the D-Day invasion in Normandy, France.

April 30, 1945
Hitler commits suicide.

May 7, 1945
Germany surrenders to the Allied forces.

August 6, 1945
A US B-29 bomber drops the first atomic bomb on Hiroshima, Japan.

August 15, 1945
Japan surrenders.

Glossary

alliances
Unions between nations for protection.

bonds
Certificates that promise payment from the government by a certain date.

chaos
Complete confusion.

communism
A system of government in which a single party controls all business and production.

democracy
A system of government in which the leaders are elected by the people.

dictator
A leader who has complete control over a country.

fascism
A political system headed by a dictator; the government controls business, and opposition is not permitted.

Holocaust
The killing of Jews and other minorities by the Nazis during World War II.

infamy
The state of being known for doing something evil.

intelligence
An agency that finds out information about the enemy.

sacrifice
To give up something for a greater cause.

For More Information

Books

Adams, Simon. *DK Eyewitness Books: World War II*. New York: DK Children, 2007.

Garland, Sherry, and Layne Johnson. *Voices of Pearl Harbor*. Gretna, LA: Pelican, 2013.

McGowen, Tom. *D-Day* (Cornerstones of Freedom: Second). New York: Children's Press, 2008.

Peppas, Lynn. *The Holocaust* (Uncovering the Past: Analyzing Primary Sources). New York: Crabtree, 2015.

Visit 12StoryLibrary.com

Scan the code or use your school's login at **12StoryLibrary.com** for recent updates about this topic and a full digital version of this book. Enjoy free access to:

- Digital ebook
- Breaking news updates
- Live content feeds
- Videos, interactive maps, and graphics
- Additional web resources

Note to educators: Visit 12StoryLibrary.com/register to sign up for free premium website access. Enjoy live content plus a full digital version of every 12-Story Library book you own for every student at your school.

Index

About the Author

Patricia Hutchison is the author of several nonfiction books about science and history for children. She was a teacher for more than 30 years. In 2014, Patricia attended the Belfer National Conference for Educators at the United States Holocaust Memorial Museum.

READ MORE FROM 12-STORY LIBRARY

Every 12-Story Library book is available in many formats. For more information, visit 12StoryLibrary.com.